DUTCH SCHULTZ
AND HIS LOST
CATSKILLS' TREASURE

Also by John Conway

*Retrospect: An Anecdotal History of
Sullivan County, New York*

DUTCH SCHULTZ AND HIS LOST CATSKILLS' TREASURE

JOHN CONWAY

PURPLE MOUNTAIN PRESS
FLEISCHMANNS, NEW YORK

To Debra, my wife and best friend, who has always shown remarkable patience for my preoccupations.

Dutch Schultz and His Lost Catskills' Treasure
First edition 2000

Published by
PURPLE MOUNTAIN PRESS, LTD.
P.O. Box 309, Fleischmanns, New York 12430-0309
845-254-4062, 845-254-4476 (fax), purple@catskill.net
http://www.catskill.net/purple

Copyright © 2000 by John Conway
All rights reserved under International and Pan-American Copyright Conventions.

No part of this book may be reproduced or transmitted in any form without permission in writing from the publisher.

ISBN 1-930098-11-1

On the cover:
Phoenicia-area map notations by a psychic from Virginia, who sought unsuccessfully to find Dutch Schultz's treasure.

The Phoenicia area is most often cited as the burial ground of the Dutchman's hoarded millions. Some versions of the legend put the loot near Route 28, along the Esopus Creek, others favor the Stony Clove Creek off Route 214 north of town.

5 4 3 2

Manufactured in the United States of America

Table of Contents

I. The Beginning
7

II. The Rise To Power
14

III. The Catskill Connection
18

IV. The Treasure
20

V. The Saga Continues
34

Appendix: The Mob In The Catskills
36

Notes
38

1. THE BEGINNING

IT is indisputable that Arthur Flegenheimer grew up to be, for a time at least, the most powerful gangster in America. He did it without flash or diplomacy. He was a straight-ahead kind of guy. That's the way he lived, and that's the way he died. There was nothing subtle about him. But for someone so frank and direct, he was always uncharacteristically vague about his childhood.

Arthur was born to Herman and Emma Flegenheimer on August 6, 1902, at 1690 Second Avenue in Manhattan and moved with his parents to the Bronx at an early age, but that's about all that is known for certain. For years, it was believed that Herman Flegenheimer had deserted the family when Arthur was eight years old, but at a news conference in the spring of 1935, Arthur himself revealed that his father had died when he was 14, refusing to discuss the matter any further. Herman Flegenheimer has been alternately described as a saloonkeeper, a glazier, a baker, and a livery operator.[1]

Mrs. Flegenheimer has been remembered by some sources as "deeply religious," and by others as "not so pious."[2] In that same news conference, Arthur maintained that his parents were not religious, and that he had never been taken to a synagogue. Still, some family acquaintances from those early days remember Mrs. Flegenheimer scraping together a few cents to purchase kosher chickens for dinner. Nonetheless, there is no indication that Arthur was ever a practicing Jew, and, in fact, he became a Catholic shortly before his death.

When the Flegenheimers settled in the lower Bronx, Arthur attended grade school at PS 12 through the sixth grade. He claimed to have been an avid student and maintained that he dropped out only because he needed to help support his mother. The truth of the matter is that he became a gang member at an early age, and despite his contention that he was a hard working youth, putting in time as a printer's devil and a roofer's helper—some have written that Schultz carried a roofer's union card on his person throughout his life as a reminder of his days as a "working man," others disdain the notion that he ever got his hands dirty in honest labor—he spent most of his time brawling with other gang members and mugging passersby. He was first arrested in 1919, but the charges were dropped for lack of evidence. Later that same year, he was convicted of breaking into a Manhattan apartment and sentenced to an indeterminate stay at Blackwell's Island in New York's East River. Far from a model inmate, he became such a problem for those running the island home for wayward boys that he was transferred to Westhampton Prison Farm near Goshen in Orange County. Apparently Arthur didn't care much for those surroundings, either; he escaped shortly

Dutch Schultz

Arthur Flegenheimer, alias Dutch Schultz, was 5'7" and weighed 175 pounds. Someone once said he looked "like Bing Crosby with a busted-up nose."

Schultz (left) with his equally crooked attorney, Richard "Dixie" Davis. Davis was later disbarred.

after arriving there, only to be recaptured before he had spent a full day on the outside. He eventually served 15 months. It was the only prison term he would ever serve.[3]

It's not clear exactly when Arthur Flegenheimer became Dutch Schultz—nor exactly how. It has been written that he was a member of the Frog Hollow Gang, a notorious group of thugs accustomed to calling their toughest member "Dutch Schultz" after a revered former leader. (Frog Hollow was a name locals used to describe an area of the Bronx around East 148th Street and Morris Avenue. The Frog Hollow Gang dated back to well before the turn of the century.) However, newspaperman Paul Sann, in his well-researched 1971 work, *Kill The Dutchman!* wrote that Arthur was a member of a rival gang, bitter enemies of the Frog Hollow group, and hints that he requisitioned the nickname "Dutch Schultz" to bolster "a never-proven reputation as a tough guy." Regardless, Arthur himself became enamored of his new sobriquet, at least in part because it was short enough to fit in the headlines. "If I'd kept the name Flegenheimer, nobody would have heard of me," he was once quoted as saying.[4]

Like fellow bootleggers Legs Diamond and Waxey Gordon, Schultz became a protege of Arnold Rothstein, Mr. Big, whose noted business acumen must have rubbed off on Schultz, who learned his trade quickly and well. Although he actually got a later start in the underworld than either Diamond or Gordon, he proved more durable and successful than either of them.[5]

Schultz also forged a number of other alliances during these early years; and while most would last just a short time, some would significantly impact the rest of his life. These alliances included Marcel Poffo, who taught Arthur the protection racket and how to heist packages off delivery trucks; Joey Noe, who became the up-and-coming gangster's first partner in a burgeoning bootlegging business; and Vincent "Mad Dog" Coll, the trigger-happy sociopath who was first a member of the same gang of tattered youths, and then later a bitter enemy who engaged in a losing shooting war with the powerful Schultz.

Each of these hoodlums met their demise before Dutch Schultz was rubbed out in 1935. Poffo's bullet-riddled body was found in Westchester County in 1933, Coll was gunned down in a drugstore phone booth—undoubtedly by Schultz's men—in 1932, and Joey Noe was killed by rival bootleggers in 1928. His death probably affected Dutch Schultz more than any other he would deal with during his lifetime. Not only was Joey Noe the Dutchman's best friend and business partner, but his death left Schultz sole owner of the lucrative booze racket they had developed together and was his undeniable springboard to bigger and badder things.[6]

Police speculated then that it was Legs Diamond's men who did Joey Noe in, though they could never prove it. Schultz must have lent some credence to that theory, though, for he would return the favor just a few years later. He was undoubtedly responsible for Diamond's murder in an Albany hotel room in 1931.

Prior to Noe's death, the inseparable pair had largely restricted their bootlegging business to the Bronx. Within a few years of his partner's untimely demise, however,

Schultz had spread out considerably, and using lead and blood, became the undisputed king of the New York City rackets. It has been written, though never proven, that a violent argument over money between the Dutchman and restaurant union leader Jules Martin was settled abruptly when Schultz drew a .45 caliber automatic from the waistband of his pants, shoved it in Martin's mouth, and blew off his head.[7]

II. THE RISE TO POWER

FEW GANGSTERS of any era were ever as resourceful as Dutch Schultz when it came to finding new ways to accumulate money without working for it. When Prohibition was repealed in 1932, the criminals who had become multi-millionaires during its tenure went scurrying about for ways to replace the lost source of income. Schultz was way ahead of them. He had already taken over the lucrative numbers racket in Harlem, traditionally run by and for the black population there. He engaged in a ruthless war with the self-proclaimed Madame Queen, Stephanie St. Claire and her cohort Ellsworth "Bumpy" Johnson for control of the Harlem operation, which at one point was estimated to earn Schultz himself some $16,000 a week.[8]

Not content with the already massive profits from the penny games, Schultz hired Otto Berman, a mathematical genius who had earned the nickname "Abbadabba" with his magical handling of numbers, to rig the results so the smallest possible payout was made each day. It was a system no one has been able to recreate since. The winning numbers in those days were taken from the results at various racetracks. Berman figured out a way to put just enough money into the pari-mutuel machines to have a lightly played number come out. The system purportedly added ten percent to the gangster's take each day.[9] This type of greed was Schultz's trademark, and all in all, he showed a particularly blatant disregard for the Harlem population, including those on his payroll, whom he called "chimney sweeps."[10]

It is a testimony to Schultz's ability as a money maker that the highly regarded mobster Meyer Lansky also realized the immense profits to be had from the Harlem numbers racket and coveted that action for his Bug and Meyer gang. But Lansky and his pal Benjamin "Bugsy" Siegel moved too slowly to infiltrate the territory—as did their close ally Charles "Lucky" Luciano—and Schultz beat them to it. Surely the fact they so relished a piece of this action influenced their ultimate decision to have Schultz killed, though without the mathematical wizardry of Otto Berman, they were never able to maximize the profits the way the Dutchman had.

The numbers racket was only part of the Dutch Schultz portfolio. He was also probably the first gangster to successfully infiltrate organized labor, eventually running both the window washers and waiters and bartenders unions. And while Frank Costello has always been known as the "Prime Minister of the Underworld" for his ability to influence law enforcement and elected officials, Schultz was a forerunner in this field, too. He was a master of the payoff, and didn't stop at public officials, either. He ingeniously "paid off" the townspeople in both Syracuse and Malone, New York prior to going on trial on income tax evasion charges in those communities, and the initial trial ended in a hung jury while the re-trial resulted in his acquittal.

This, despite a well earned reputation as a skin-flint. Schultz was so cheap, he even cheated his own men. Another of Otto Berman's duties was to "adjust" the weekly payroll so the Dutchman's overhead could be kept to a minimum. It was a well-known fact that he paid his gunmen less than the going rate. Only Berman got top dollar—about $10,000 a week—and then only because he threatened to take his skills elsewhere.

Unlike other successful gangsters of his era, Schultz shunned fancy clothes and fast cars. He once told a newspaperman that "only queers wear silk shirts," an undoubted dig at his rivals. "I never bought one in my life," he claimed. "A guy's a sucker to spend fifteen or twenty dollars on a shirt. Hell, a guy can get a good one for two bucks."

This unabashed cheapness irritated his fellow gangsters. Lucky Luciano once called Schultz "the cheapest guy I ever knew." Luciano said Schultz dressed like a pig. "He worried about spending two cents for a newspaper," Charley Lucky said. "That was his big spending, buying the papers so he could read about himself."[11]

Still, his miserly ways did not stop the Dutchman from spreading around the cash when he felt it would help keep him out of a jam. In 1938, Schultz's long-time attorney, Richard "Dixie" Davis would testify that at the Dutchman's direction he paid off Tammany Hall leader James J. Hines "15 or 20 times" to act as guardian angel of the gang's numbers racket. "If Jimmy should ask for anything, give it to him within reason. We will get it back from the numbers game." Davis says Schultz once told him.[12]

Schultz became so big that, when Lucky Luciano and Meyer Lansky decided to organize the premier gangsters of the era into "the Combination" or "the Syndicate," it was necessary that the Dutchman be included. Together with Luciano, Lansky, Louis "Lepke" Buchalter, Frank Costello, Joe Adonis, and Abner "Longy" Zwillman, he sat on the board of directors of the newly formed crime corporation. The concept of the Syndicate was one of cooperation, and the understanding was that no one would take any major steps to expand their territory or to remove a competitor without the consent of the board. Of course, the greedy Schultz had never been much of a team player, and the others were well aware of his reputation as a loose cannon, so he was usually the odd man out when votes were taken. The alliance was a shaky one, and one which would prove to be the Dutchman's ultimate undoing.

III. THE CATSKILL CONNECTION

ALL HIS OTHER ENTERPRISES notwithstanding, it was Prohibition that brought Dutch Schultz to the Catskills. Like many of the bootleggers of the day, he appreciated the privacy the remote, desolate area offered, and he recognized the value in controlling a piece of land on a direct route from Canada to New York City. He established a hideout in Phoenicia sometime during the mid-1920s, and operated several stills nearby. Nearly 70 years later many local residents still remembered Schultz and spoke of him in hushed, almost reverential tones.

A Phoenicia old-timer named Mickey Simpson used to see Schultz in town from time to time. Once he happened upon one of the gangster's bootlegging trucks, crippled by a flat tire. Like any good neighbor, Simpson pulled over to help. He changed the truck's tire, with the help of the hydraulic jack that had come with his new Oldsmobile, under the watchful stare of Dutch's machine-gun toting thugs.

"That was the fastest tire I ever changed," Simpson recalled in 1991.[13] Some old-timers insist Schultz owned property in the area—a stretch along Muddy Brook is most often mentioned—though no records have been found to support that contention. Of course, it's possible that any land the Dutchman purchased could have been recorded under any of a dozen aliases he used—Joseph Harmon, Charles Harmon, and Arthur Schultz were just a few—recorded under a cohort's name, or not recorded at all. Other locals claim he used an old farm just outside of town as a hideout when the heat was particularly unbearable in the city. Regardless, there is little disagreement about the fact that Schultz and his men were seen in the area on a fairly regular basis, and some old-timers even point out pieces of rusting sheet metal along Baker Road in West Hurley, not far south of Phoenicia they claim are the remnants of one of the Dutchman's many local distilleries.

The Ulster County newspapers of the day occasionally recorded accounts of gun battles waged on the back roads and bridges between Schultz's men and those working for rival bootlegger Legs Diamond, headquartered at Friedman's Shady Lawn Hotel in nearby Highland. Those same papers ran periodic editorials in which they urged local citizens and law enforcement to clamp down on the out-of-town gangsters, but even in the 1920s, both Diamond and Schultz were much too big, and much too shrewd for that. In fact, even a relentless and seasoned racket buster like Thomas E. Dewey had trouble pinning a rap on the Dutchman and making it stick.

IV. THE TREASURE

IT was during the time that Federal Prosecutor Thomas E. Dewey was pursuing him on income tax evasion charges that Dutch Schultz decided to take an unusual precaution. He had seen many of his contemporaries put away for various terms in prison, only to come out without a dime and with their former territories taken over by rival thugs, and he was determined to avoid a similar fate. So it was that he ordered his henchmen to gather up the millions he had hoarded over the years and stash it away for the proverbial rainy day. Just what form this cache of wealth took is not clear, nor is the actual amount Schultz was able to scrape together. Some accounts of the story say his nest egg was all in currency, other accounts have it as double-eagle gold pieces, while still others describe it as a combination of cash, gold, and jewels. Likewise, some versions of the story put the value of the stash at $5 million, while other versions claim it was $7 or even $9 million. Whatever the amount, this hoarded loot was supposedly gathered into tobacco sacks and stuffed in either an iron box or steel suitcases and hidden away—buried, if you will—to be claimed at a later date.

It was only upon Schultz's death that the existence of this treasure was made known, and then only under the most incredible of circumstances.

Even after he had been acquitted on the federal tax charges in the Malone trial, Schultz found himself doggedly pursued by Dewey for other crimes. Finally, in 1935, he decided that only Dewey's death would put an end to the pursuit, and he devised a plan to knock the prosecutor off. Before carrying out this daring deed, however, Schultz met with the other top level gangsters on the board of directors of the Syndicate to apprise them of his plan. Luciano and Lansky were astute enough to realize that murdering a man of Dewey's stature would bring down considerable heat on their lucrative operations and cost them millions of dollars, so they persuaded the others to vote against Schultz's proposition. This infuriated the Dutchman, who vowed to carry out the assassination on his own. "I don't need your permission," he angrily announced, and stormed out of the meeting.[14]

That fit of temper was enough to convince Luciano and Lansky that Schultz was even more unstable than they had initially believed, and coupled with their own desire to take over the Dutchman's profitable rackets, sealed Schultz's fate. The Syndicate would eliminate Schultz and his gang before they could eliminate Dewey.

Because of the relentless heat Dewey had succeeded in bringing to bear on him in the city, Schultz had fled across the river to Newark, New Jersey, where he had set up shop in the Palace Chop House, a working-class tavern and restaurant with a low profile. A team of killers led by Charles "Bug" Workman was dispatched to that location, and on October 23, 1935, a hail of bullets rid the world of Dutch Schultz, Otto Berman, and bodyguards Lulu Rosenkranz and Abe Landau.

Schultz had excused himself from the business meeting in his office just moments before Workman entered the Chop House and was washing his hands when the assassin routinely checked the room for witnesses. Not recognizing Schultz, the Bug let out a burst of machine gun fire at the man at the sink just as a precaution, and proceeded to the office where he quickly and coldly dispatched the others.

Schultz had been hit in the spleen, stomach, colon and liver. He was mortally wounded, but he didn't die right away. Rushed to Newark City Hospital following the massacre, he lingered for nearly 24 hours, and drifted in and out of consciousness. His insides had been destroyed, and the ensuing infection ran his fever up to 106 degrees. The resulting delirium caused a steady stream of chatter, and police stenographer John Long was assigned to write down every word. It wasn't long before the dying words of Dutch Schultz made their way into the newspapers, and everyone in the world soon knew about the existence of the Dutchman's stashed millions.

Although there are a number of slightly different versions of Schultz's dying words, none contain much more than disjointed, incoherent ramblings. One version that is often reproduced begins *Oh, mama, mama, mama...I am a pretty good pretzler...How many shots were fired at me?...*

John, please, did you buy me the hotel for a million?...I'll get you the cash out of the box...there's enough in it to buy four-five more...You can play jacks and girls do that with a soft ball and do tricks with...Lulu, drive me back to Phoenicia...Don't be a dope Lulu, we better get those Liberty bonds out of the box and cash 'em...sure it was Danny's mistake to buy 'em and I think they can be traced...Danny please get me in the car...Kindly take my shoes off, they're not off...there's handcuffs on 'em... Wonder who owns these woods?...he'll never know what's hidden in 'em...My gilt-edge stuff and those rats have tuned in...What did that guy shoot me for?[15]

Other versions contain additional references such as *Please crack down on the Chinaman's friends and Hitler's commander...All right, I am sore and I am going up and I am going to give you honey if I can...Look out...We broke that up...Mother is the best bet and don't let Satan draw you too fast...*[16]

Soon, there were as many versions of the legend of the buried treasure as there were stories of the Dutchman himself. Most of them involved Phoenicia, and many referenced a map, supposedly sketched by Lulu Rosenkranz lest the location of the burial site be forgotten by the city slickers still strangers to the trees and rocks and streams of the upstate country.

Several versions of the treasure tale place the location of the burial ground somewhere along Route 28 between the roadway and the Esopus Creek. Some place it along the railroad tracks leading into Phoenicia. One of the most popular stories is that Schultz and Lulu Rosenkranz carried a steel safe containing the loot to Phoenicia on an April night in 1933 and buried it in a grove of pine trees near the Esopus, with the obligatory "X" marking the specific tree under which the digging was done.[17]

A more elaborate version of the events surrounding the hiding of the loot was revealed nearly 50 years ago by an old-timer—he was over 80 years old at the time—who claimed to have first-hand knowledge of the day Schultz and his men found a home for their millions.

This account has the treasure being buried the very afternoon Schultz and his gang were ambushed at the Palace Chop House. According to this tale, Dutch and one of his men, probably Rosenkranz, stopped for lunch at the Phoenicia Hotel, in the center of town. They left around one o'clock, got in a car, and drove a half a block, where they made a right hand turn onto Route 214. They proceeded north along the Stony Clove Creek for about eight miles, and stashed the money beneath the skull-shaped rock formation known as the Devil's Face. The two men were back in Phoenicia by three o'clock that afternoon, and returned to Newark for their fateful rendezvous with Bug Workman that evening.[18]

Schultz's deathbed ramblings did make a reference or two to Satan, so the connection to the Devil's Face formation is a logical one, though it would seem more likely that the landmark Schultz would have used is the large rock known as the Devil's Tombstone, which is closer to town, and considerably more accessible than the 150-foot high rock skull. These were city boys, after all.

The late Mickey Simpson, a Phoenicia old-timer who remembered Schultz as well as anyone, had his own theory about the treasure. Sure, he said in 1991, Schultz might have buried his loot by the Esopus Creek, but if he did it was long gone. The Phoenicia area had suffered a number of serious floods over the years, he said, and surely even an iron box couldn't have survived them all. "Personally, I wouldn't step off this porch for it," Simpson said. "It's probably somewhere at the bottom of the Ashokan Reservoir."[19]

Locals also like to tell stories of the elderly man who used to walk from place to place along the railroad tracks digging holes. When asked what he was digging for, he would say simply, "Dutch Schultz's buried treasure." The railroad finally made him stop; he was destroying their ballast.

A Phoenicia motel operator used to allow treasure hunters to dig on his property, but first asked them to sign a legal document promising him a split of whatever they found there. He abruptly stopped the practice when a particularly resourceful treasure hunter showed up with a backhoe, dug dozens of holes, and disappeared without filling them back in.

A different account of the legend comes from an Alexandria, Virginia, man who claims he was guided to Phoenicia by the ethereal revelations of the long dead Otto Berman, who had been destined to an eternity of unrest until the surviving ill-gotten gains of his criminal career were turned over to the poor children of the Bronx. This man had never heard of Otto Berman and had only the vaguest notion of who Dutch Schultz was, when he happened upon a television account of the buried treasure some ten years ago. He found himself uncharacteristically drawn to the story and couldn't get it out of his head. Soon he was researching accounts of Schultz's life and death and became convinced that he was being prodded and guided by some other-worldly voice, which he later determined to be Berman's. In fact, he claims to have had visions of the night the treasure was hidden, visions he believes are the scenes Berman himself saw while watching Schultz and two others ditch the booty.

In this unique account of the treasure tale, on September 10, 1935, just over a month before he was killed, Schultz decided to stash his fortune until after he murdered Dewey. He was apparently planning to reclaim it after Dewey was hit, and make his getaway, to another country if necessary. According to the visions, the money, encased in an iron box 16" wide by 24" long, was placed two feet below the surface in a four-foot-diameter hole next to the Stony Clove Creek, behind a Main Street rooming house where Schultz and his men stayed. The man claims to have seen dirt from the hole, which he thinks was dug where the rooming house owners burned their garbage, being shoveled into the creek. Since the men burying the treasure were already extremely familiar with the backyard location where it was placed, no maps or sketches or written descriptions of the hiding place were necessary, and none was made.

Next two pages: **From the notes of the Virginia man who was led to Phoenicia by psychic visions he believed were seen through the eyes of Otto "Abbadabba" Berman. A sketch of the iron box in which the treasure was supposedly buried is included.**

Dutch Schultz

19 October 1994

It occured to me while walking Keisha this evening that I've never bothered to put down a description of the placement of the chest in the burial hole. It also occured to me that the round shaped thing the chest was beneath wasn't a laurel bush — maybe it was that iron kettle I unearthed partially on location by the third (standing dead) tree. It was only a foot or less buried, the chest is between (18") and (2) ft. below the surface

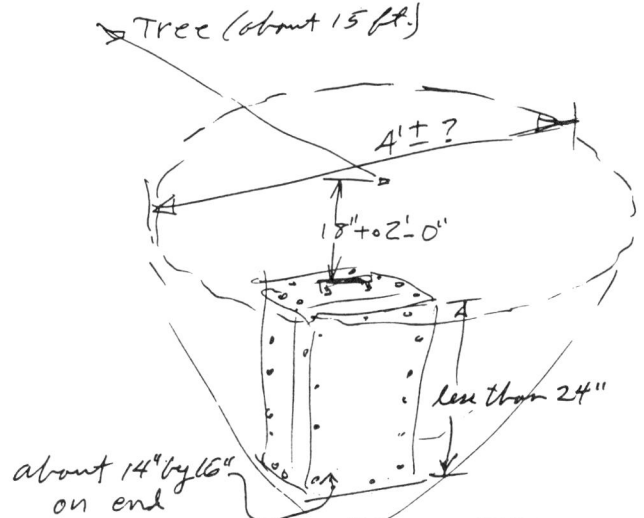

If the soil is as sandy as it appeared to be, this makes sense in retrospect. (Though I keep seeing a gray, very fine, silty, clay soil as in a coniferous woods.)

Lost Treasures of New York State

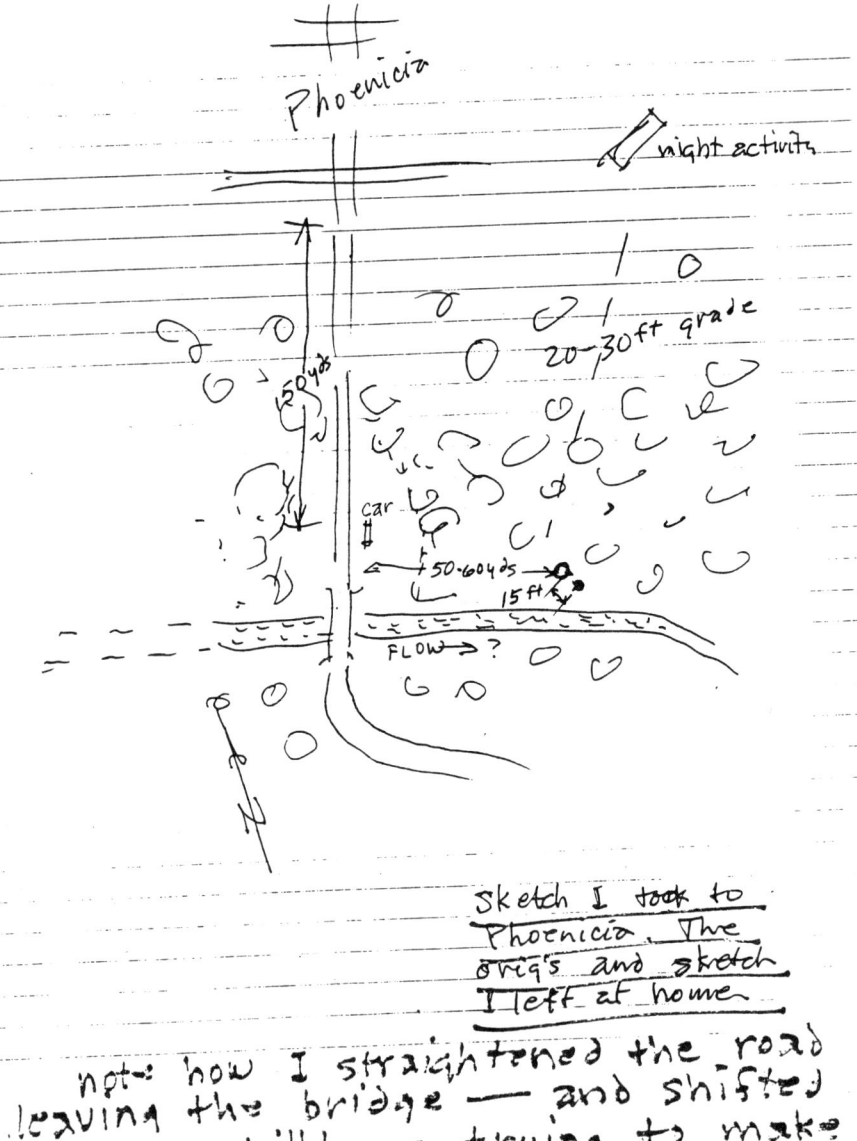

Sketch I took to Phoenicia. The orig's and sketch I left at home.

note how I straightened the road leaving the bridge — and shifted North a little — trying to make site #1 fit (before I got there)

This man was a cartographer by trade, and he felt that was the reason he was chosen for Berman's channeling. With his map-making skills, he could plot Berman's recollections on a map and locate the money for distribution to the descendants of the poor people Schultz and his men had taken advantage of by fixing the numbers games. Despite extensive research during several years working on the quest, clear visions of what Berman saw, and a number of fairly accurate maps he drew without ever having seen the area, the man was unable to find the right spot in two trips to Phoenicia.[20]

It is interesting to note, though, that the man's visions clearly indicated the Stony Clove Creek, a church within sight of the burial spot, and the presence of a fire in the vicinity of the spot the digging was done—hence his supposition that it was the place the rooming house burned its garbage. The Devil's Tombstone is located along the Stony Clove Creek, and perhaps it translated into a vision of a churchyard, for in 1893, a forest fire raged through the area where both the Devil's Tombstone and the Devil's Face are located. And, today the area is a well-known state-owned campground. Not exactly a rooming house, but in the ball park.

Another interesting version of the legend involves a map Lulu Rosenkranz is said to have sketched the night the treasure was buried. In this account, Rosenkranz gave the map to another Schultz underling, Marty Krompier, for safekeeping. Krompier was one of Schultz's most trusted men, but did not generally travel with the Dutchman and his inner circle. He managed some financial affairs for the

Schultz underling Marty Krompier figures prominently in a popular version of the legend of the buried treasure.

gang, including a number of mediocre prizefighters they controlled.

Krompier was far from the brightest hood, and his idea of keeping the map in a safe place was to carry it around in his wallet everywhere he went. When word of the hoarded millions—and the map Lulu had sketched—spread throughout the underworld in the days following Schultz's death, more than one mobster set his sights on the money. One was Jacob Shapiro, a close associate of Louis "Lepke" Buchalter, who had himself spent time vacationing in the Catskills—at the many Jewish hotels in Sullivan County. Shapiro, who was the brawn to Lepke's brain, was nicknamed "Gurrah," because his favorite expression, "get outta here!" sounded more like "gurrah da here!" when uttered through his clenched teeth. He heard that the Schultz treasure was hidden in the Catskills, and he figured he'd have a pretty good chance of recovering it. After all, he reasoned, he'd spent years in the area, and had numerous contacts there. All he needed was the map and some time, and he'd be a rich man.

Shapiro knew Krompier would be loyal to Schultz, even after his death, so he decided the map had to be taken from him by force, which meant Krompier would have to be killed. Depending upon the version of the tale to which you subscribe, Shapiro either dispatched a crew to kill Krompier, or he went to do it himself. Either way, the hapless gangster was cornered in a Manhattan barbershop while awaiting a shave, and killed. The map was retrieved from his wallet, along with an undisclosed amount of cash, which was unceremoniously flung in the stunned barber's face.

Lost Treasures of New York State

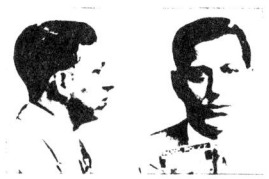

Jacob "Gurrah" Shapiro and Louis "Lepke" Buchalter were rival gangsters who coveted the lucrative rackets Schultz had developed. Lepke became *public enemy number one* following Schultz's death.

"Here's Marty's last tip," he was reportedly told. "It's a big one."

But the map proved to be a major disappointment to Shapiro. True, he had spent years vacationing in the Catskills, but in Sullivan County, not Ulster. While he expected to see places like Monticello, South Fallsburg, and Loch Sheldrake outlined on the map, he instead was looking at Phoenicia and Mount Tremper and the Esopus Creek. Enraged that he had apparently been misled, he bellowed, "these ain't the Catskills!" and tore the map to shreds, unaware of the geography lesson he had just been given.[21]

While there may be some truth to this aspect of the legend, it isn't entirely accurate. Krompier was ambushed in a Manhattan barbershop just over an hour after Schultz was shot, and although suffering several serious wounds, didn't die. The newspapers of the day speculated, as did the police, that Krompier was hit as part of a comprehensive plan to eliminate all of Schultz's men. Paul Sann provides a fairly detailed account of the episode in his book, and leaves little doubt that a hit squad dispatched by Lucky Luciano to clean up the Schultz mess, and not Gurrah Shapiro, was responsible for the attempt on Krompier's life.[22]

V. THE SAGA CONTINUES

So what's the real story of the Dutch Schultz treasure? Was there ever really millions stashed away for safekeeping? Or was it all just the fanciful imagination of some underworld thug or bored newspaperman? It's difficult to know for certain.

Hundreds of treasure hunters have tried their hands at locating the elusive loot over the years, and dozens of different methods have been employed. It's a pilgrimage that continues to this day. Some come armed with maps they say have been handed down from someone who knew someone who knew Schultz. Others have maps they say they have purchased at garage sales. And some have no maps at all, just an inkling where the booty might have been stashed. Some are serious treasure hunters, some just out for fun. Metal detectors, divining rods, shovels, crowbars, and even backhoes have been used to dig.[23] All to no avail. At least as far as anyone knows. But then again, would whoever locates the treasure let the world know, or would they keep it to themselves, fearful that it would be claimed by others or by the government?

Dutch Schultz

It is clear to anyone who has studied his life that Dutch Schultz was frugal enough to hoard the millions he is said to have stashed away, and he was most certainly flaky enough to have buried it somewhere. Whether or not it could have survived so many years without detection, though, is another matter.

We may never know for sure.

Appendix: The Mob in the Catskills

Dutch Schultz might have been the most colorful gangster of the 1920s and '30s with ties to the Catskills, but he certainly wasn't the only one. Here's a rundown on some of the others:

Jack "Legs" Diamond, one of Dutch Schultz's bitterest enemies, controlled much of the distribution of illegal booze between New York City and Albany. Diamond kept hideouts at the Shady Lawn Hotel in Highland in Ulster County and at Acra in Greene County until his death in Albany in 1931.

Waxey Gordon, born Irving Wexler, he was another of Schultz's bootlegging rivals. He spent considerable time in Sullivan County, where some say he owned a home, and may have been a partner in a small hotel in White Lake. Gordon was on the lam from the law following his indictment on income tax evasion—a charge pinned on him with the help of fellow mobsters who were out to gain control of his holdings—when he was arrested in White Lake in 1933.

Abe Reles, Pittsburgh Phil Strauss, and other members of Brooklyn's infamous Murder, Inc., the enforcement arm of the syndicate, not only frequented the posh Sullivan County resorts of the 1930s—no doubt keeping an eye on the slot machines they'd placed in many of them—but used area lakes to dump the victims of their rub-outs on more than one occasion. No fewer than eight murders in Sullivan County were traced to the efforts of Murder, Inc., when their operation began to unravel in 1939.

Walter Sage had earned admission to Murder, Inc. by rubbing out small-time hoodlum Red Alpert on a Brooklyn street corner in 1933, and eventually won a promotion to manager of the group's Sullivan County slot machines. He became a well-known figure at many of the county's resorts. When it was discovered that he had been diverting some of the profits into is own pocket, he turned up dead. His body floated to the surface of Swan Lake, just outside Liberty, during the summer of 1937. It had been lashed to a slot machine frame.

Louis "Lepke" Buchalter, Public Enemy Number One following Schultz's death, frequented the Jewish resorts of Sullivan County. He was a familiar sight at such well-known area hotels as the President in Swan Lake, the Ambassador in Fallsburg, and the Plaza in South Fallsburg.

Jacob "Gurrah" Shapiro, he of the odd-ball nickname, spent many summers vacationing in Sullivan County. He was introduced to the famous Borscht Belt resorts by his labor-racketeering friend, Lepke.

Murder, Inc. also kept a hideout in Milton, in Ulster county. A secluded tomato farm there provided a haven for many notorious killers over the years, including "the Lord High Executioner" himself, **Albert Anastasia**.

Notes

1. Paul Sann, *Kill the Dutchman!* Arlington House, 1971.
2. Several similar articles, including some in treasure-hunting magazines, have referenced Mrs. Flegenheimer's religious fervor. It appears to have been a single mistake that has been perpetuated.
3. Carl Sifakis, *The Mafia Encyclopedia*, Facts on File Publishing, 1988.
4. Ibid.
5. Ibid.
6. Sann.
7. This scene is played out in the historical novel *Billy Bathgate* by E. L. Doctorow and in the movie by the same name. There is some reason to believe it never happened. Martin was shot following an argument with Schultz but probably by Bo Weinberg, and he didn't die right away.
8. Sann.
9. Carl Sifakis, *The Encyclopedia of American Crime*, section on Otto Berman.
10. Sann.
11. Sifakis, *The Mafia Encyclopedia*.
12. *New York Journal-American*, August 31, 1938.
13. *Times Herald-Record, Sunday Magazine*, July 21, 1991.
14. Sifakis, *The Mafia Encyclopedia*.
15. Emile C. Schumacher, *Lost Treasures and How to Find Them*, Paperback Library, 1968. Rex Ladd, "Dutch Schultz's Missing $7 Million Cache," *Treasure World Magazine*, Feb.-Mar. 1973.
16. Sann. William S. Burroughs, *The Last Words of Dutch Schultz*. Seaver Books, 1975.

17 Patricia Edwards Clyne, *Hudson Valley Tales and Trails*, The Overlook Press, 1990.
18 Personal correspondence from Andrew J. Horvath, April 22, 1991.
19 *Times Herald-Record.*
20 Notes detailing the man's work were forwarded to me with correspondence from Lonnie Gale of Phoenicia, May 25, 2000.
21. Schumacher and Ladd.
22 Sann.
23 Personal interviews with Phoenicia townspeople, 1991.

A nineteenth-century forest fire in the area around the Devil's Tombstone and the Devil's Face is commemorated with a historic marker. One treasure hunter saw fire as an important clue. Here the author tries his luck there with a metal detector.